I Go Up and Down

Written by Max Greene
Illustrated by Elizabeth Traynor

Scott Foresman

I can go up the flower.

I can eat at the flower.

I can go down the flower.

I can go up the leaf.

I can eat at the leaf.

I can go down the leaf.

I can go up the tree.

I can eat at the tree.

I can go down the tree.

Now, I can sleep.